THE

OF HOW

by Sidonie Matsner Gruenberg

WITH ILLUSTRATIONS BY HILDEGARD WOODWARD

DOUBLEDAY & COMPANY, INC., GARDEN CITY, N. Y.

WONDERFUL STORY YOU WERE BORN

For my grandchildren:

PETER BARNARD	KATHERYN MARY
DANIEL BARNARD	JEAN ALLÉE
NICHOLAS BENJAMIN	JUDITH SIDONIE
ELIZABETH ALLÉE	JOEL WILLIAM
RICHARD JOSEPH	MATTHEW ALAN
ANN MATSNER	RICHARD MATSNER

and my great-grandchildren:

JOSHUA DAVID
DAVID MARK

Acknowledgments: I want to express my deep appreciation for all the help I have received in the development of this exacting little book: To my husband, Benjamin C. Gruenberg, with whom I have worked very closely on this book; to Helen Puner who collaborated with me in the preparation of the manuscript; to my colleagues at the Child Study Association of America for many helpful suggestions; and to Dr. Grace McLean Abbate for her wise counsel.

Many years ago . . .

. . . when I was very young, young as you are now, I used to wonder about many things. I wondered what made the rain rain, where the sky ended, and where the light went when the dark began. But most of all I wondered where I came from. "Where was I before I was born?" I wondered. "How did I begin?" "How did I get born?"

I wanted to know the answer to these questions very much. I think all children do. I mean, I *know* all children do. For I am a grandmother now—my four children have eleven children of their own. And when my children were as young as you are now, they asked me these same questions. And their children asked *them* these same questions—just as I did, just as they did, just as you are asking now.

"Where did I come from?" "How was I born?" Children all over the world have always asked these same questions. But when I was a little girl, most parents didn't think it wise to answer. You see, in those days, most parents believed that children could not understand the real story of where babies come from.

So when I tried to find out, I got some very queer answers.

When I asked my father, he told me to ask my mother. When I asked my mother, she told me to wait until I was older.

My friends were shy and giggly when I asked them, and each one told me something different. Emily said her mother told her that she'd been found under a cabbage leaf. Janey's parents said they had ordered *her* from a big store. Bobby said he had been brought by a big white stork. Marian was brought by a fairy her mother had known as a girl; at least, that's what she'd been *told*. All of these were just made-up stories.

But the really true story of where babies come from is far more interesting and surprising

It is part of the whole story of how *all* living things keep on coming into the world. For not only does every person have a beginning. So do all kinds of living things around us—the birds and fish and other animals, the trees and bushes and grass.

People wonder about this old story more than about any other they've ever heard. It is always new to every one of us. My children and grandchildren often wondered about it, so I have answered many, many questions over many years, and now I would like to tell *you* the true story of how babies are born.

At the beginning of you, you were no bigger than a dot—a tiny dot, much smaller even than the dot on this page. Smaller than the point of a pin, or the dot a pencil makes on paper, or a single grain of sand. So small that the dot could not be seen at all, except through a strong magnifying glass. The dot that was going to be you was like a tiny little round egg. And that is what you really were—a tiny, tiny little egg.

Everybody you know started to be and started to grow from just such an egg. Your mother did and your father did, and your sisters and your brothers, and your cousins and your teachers and your friends. No matter how big anyone is now or how small, he began in exactly the same way. No matter whether a person has white skin, or brown skin, or yellow skin, whether he lives in America, or India, or Africa, or China, he began as a tiny little egg.

Everything else on earth that's alive started out as a tiny dot of an egg, too. All the furry animals you know —from the biggest bears to the smallest mice. Yes, and the crickets and the flies, the frogs and the fish, and every kind of plant and vegetable and tree—all of these started from a tiny dot-sized egg. In most plants, these eggs grow into seeds.

But even though every living thing began from a little dot, each one is different. Each new plant and each new animal grows to be the same kind of living thing as its parents.

I once knew a little girl whose mother was going to have a baby. The family already had three children, but no pets. So this little girl thought it would be more fun if her mother had a kitten instead of a baby.

Of course, her mother *couldn't* have had a kitten. People can have only human children like yourself and your friends. Dogs can have only puppies, and cats only kittens. Pine trees can make only the seeds that grow into other pine trees, and robins only the eggs that grow into robins.

So, the tiny little dot that you began from was a very special and wonderful kind of little egg. It couldn't have grown into a puppy, or a bunny, or a cucumber. It couldn't have grown into a kangaroo, or a cockatoo, or a duck-billed platypus. It could only have grown into a human being like you.

There's another thing about the egg that's just as special and wonderful. That's this: even though the egg was as tiny as a dot, it had in it nearly everything that it took to make *you*. You, with your knees and your elbows, and your eyelashes and your fingernails. You, with your questions and giggles, your tears and kisses. You, with your way of growing from a tiny baby sleeping all day in a crib, to a big boy or girl going to school and learning to read and write.

Your being able to grow from something very small and helpless into something pretty big and independent was right there in the tiny egg you began from!

Isn't that amazing? I know that even though I'm a grandmother my wonder about it never stops.

From the time you started to grow, the egg that was you lay inside a special place in your mother's body. This place is called the womb, or uterus. It is shaped like a pear and is well below her stomach. That's where you lived for nine whole months—the time it takes for all human babies to get big enough to be born.

All this time you needed food and you needed air— for you were alive, even though you weren't yet born.

You got the food and you got the air through a kind of cord that connected your body with the inside of your mother's womb. Of course you didn't taste roast beef and butterscotch pudding the way you do now. But you *did* get all the special kinds of food and the air you needed for growing.

Your mother's womb was the first home you ever had. A mother's womb is a fine place for an unborn baby. It keeps the baby warm even if the mother walks through an ice storm. For the inside of the womb is always warm, just like other parts of the human body. And it's always the same warmth—just right for the baby.

The unborn baby isn't easily bumped or banged, even if the mother should get bumped or banged. For the baby inside the womb lies curled up in a bag of watery fluid. And this fluid acts like a springy cushion between the baby and any bump or shake-up the mother might accidentally get.

The tiny dot that was you grew larger and larger—and larger. And as it grew, it slowly began to change its shape. After a few weeks of growing, you looked something like a funny little curled-up fish. But you were still very small, no larger than a tiny pebble.

After growing inside your mother's body a few weeks more, you were about an inch long and rather strange looking.

So you kept on growing month after month. You kept on changing your shape. Soon you began to look more and more like the babies you've seen. Tiny arms and legs pushed out, eyes and ears and nose appeared. All the parts that make up a born baby, a complete human being, were growing into place.

13

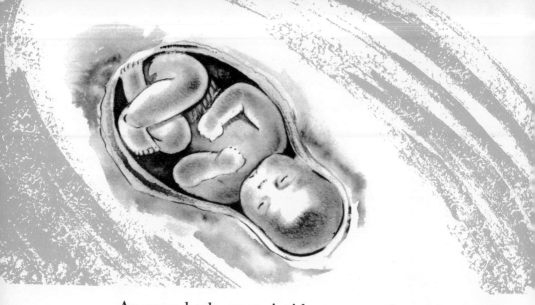

As your body grew inside your mother, her womb stretched and grew, too, so there was always room for you. Your mother's breasts also grew larger. They were filling with milk that you would need after you were born.

And after about four or five months of growing—about as long as from Thanksgiving to Easter, or from the Fourth of July to Hallowe'en—you began to stir and move a little inside your mother's body. From the tiny, still egg you had been, you had grown and changed so much in this time that you were able to move your arms and legs! No, your stirring and moving didn't hurt your mother. She was pleased and excited when you fluttered about inside her. And this gave her one of the happiest, most wonderful feelings a mother has.

14

Your mother knew that in a few more months you would be ready to be born. She knew that then she would have either a little girl or a little boy of her own. Your father and mother waited eagerly for the great day to come when you would be born!

Everybody in the family was waiting to see what you would be like. Would you be a girl or a boy? Would you have light hair or dark hair—or hardly enough hair to show any color? Would you look like your mother or like your father—or a little bit like both of them?

All your family had presents ready to give you. A special place with your own little bed and your own towels and soap was waiting for you. And special clothes that looked like dolls' clothes were waiting for you to wear.

And while everybody was getting ready for you, you were getting ready for the great day, and your mother's body was getting ready, too.

A baby lies in the womb with his head near a passage in his mother's body that leads to the outside. This narrow passage is called the *vagina*.

When the time came for you to leave your mother's body, an amazing thing began to happen. The walls of her womb had been stretching and stretching as you were growing. And then—when you were ready to be born—they stopped stretching. Instead, they began to push the baby that was you down into the vagina. The vagina, too, stretched. From the vagina you got outside your mother's body—and so into the world. That's the moment you were born!

Some babies take longer to get born than others. Some take only a few hours, others take a whole day or more. Have you ever heard your mother say whether you took a long time or a short time to be born?

Most babies are born in a hospital because this is a convenient place for mother and baby to get all the attention they need. But this doesn't mean that the mothers are sick. There are other reasons why mothers go to hospitals to have their babies.

For one thing, a mother needs a doctor and nurse to help her while her baby is being born. For another thing, it sometimes hurts a mother to give birth to a baby. And a doctor and nurse can help to make the pain less.

Many mothers don't mind the pain at all. I know this sounds funny to you. But giving birth to a baby is such a wonderful and special thing for a mother that the joy she feels is much stronger than the pain. Your mother

17

was happy because she was about to see her baby for the first time—the baby who was you, who had been alive but unseen inside her for so many months.

Another reason for a doctor to be there is to take care of the baby after he is born and to listen for his first cry. Your first cry told the doctor that you were ready and able to breathe all by yourself.

The doctor also cuts the cord through which you got your food and air while you were in the womb. For a born baby is ready to take food through his mouth and to breathe through his nose and lungs all by himself. And the place where the doctor cut the cord made a little round button in the middle of your belly—the belly button, which is called the navel. No, it doesn't hurt the mother when the cord is cut, or the baby either.

Then the doctor held you up for your mother to see. You were a real born baby now. And your mother and father were very, very happy. They told everybody all about you—how much you weighed, what your name was and how proud they were that you had come to be their own little baby. Perhaps they sent out cards telling about you to all of the family and all of their friends. Maybe the little cards had a picture of a stork carrying a baby! That's because of that old story that people used to tell children about how a stork brought them. It was told for so long—for hundreds and hundreds of years— that the stork has come to stand for birth. And it always makes people smile. Besides, it makes a pretty picture.

JUNE 4th

BILL JR.
7 pounds

So—now you know how you lived in your mother's body before you were born, and how you grew from a tiny egg to be a baby.

But . . .

. . . it takes a father as well as a mother to start this baby.

You know that every baby is born either a boy or a girl—that is, either male or female. You know that boys grow up to be men and girls grow to be women. You also know that the bodies of boys and the bodies of girls are different from each other. A boy or a man has a penis, and a girl or a woman has a vagina. Both males and females have other parts *inside* their bodies that have to do with making babies. All these parts we call *sex organs*.

The sex organs inside a girl or woman are the womb and two special parts that make the tiny eggs. They are called *ovaries*. Each ovary is about as thick as a grown-up's thumb. These two special parts are able to make hundreds of eggs.

Every month a single egg leaves one of the two ovaries and travels down a tube leading to the womb, which is close by. In the mother's womb the egg is ready to begin to grow into a baby. But only if it is joined by something else.

This very important something is called a *sperm*, and it comes from the father's body.

A father's body is very different from a mother's. The father has a pair of special sex organs that make sperms.

They are inside a bag hanging just below the penis and are called *testicles*. A man's testicles make millions of sperms, but only one single sperm melts with an egg into a living, growing being.

You may find this hard to imagine, but the sperm that makes it possible for the egg to grow into a baby is even smaller than the egg—very much smaller! It's so tiny that nobody has even seen one, except through a *very* strong magnifying glass.

Through a magnifying glass, a sperm looks something like the tadpoles you may have seen in brooks or ponds in the spring. It has a long, thin, wiggling tail and a roundish little head. It swims about like a tadpole, too, with quick wrigglings of its tail.

As soon as a sperm meets an egg, something amazing

happens. The tiny little egg made in the mother's body, and the tiny little sperm from the father's body, *melt together*. They are no longer two separate things. They have become *one new* thing. That one new thing is the egg combined with the sperm, and it is really very different from the egg by itself. We call it a *fertilized egg*. It is this new thing that becomes a baby.

The little egg in your mother's body, by itself, was not you. And the little sperm in your father's body, by itself, wasn't you. *You* began to be only when the two joined together. That was the moment you started to be yourself. That was the moment when you became able to grow into a baby, and after that into a boy or girl, and after that into a man or woman.

In that first moment when the sperm and the egg joined to make you, the question of whether you were going to be a girl or boy was settled. That, and many, many other things—even the color of your hair and the color of your eyes.

Yes, all of these things were settled right there in the tiny egg at that moment when a sperm and an egg united! That's another reason why, even though I am a grandmother, I'm still full of wonder at the marvelous story of birth.

You began, then, only when something from your father's body joined something from your mother's body.

The sperms come from the father's body through his penis. Waste water, or urine, passes through the penis, too; but urine and sperms never pass through at the same time. A man's penis can fit into a woman's vagina, that passage in her body that ends in an opening between the legs. In this way the sperm enters the body of the mother. They can swim up the vagina through the womb and into the tubes. In one of these a sperm might join an egg moving toward the womb.

You have a mother and a father. And everybody you know had a mother and father. That's because they all began when a sperm and an egg joined. The sperm came from the father and the egg from the mother. That's why you may have brown eyes like your father, but blond hair like your mother. That is why we may say you "take after" your father in some ways, even though you have grown inside your mother's body. That is why you could have a dimpled chin like your mother, and a good singing voice like your father.

Sometimes people may even say you are "the image of" your grandfather. Or your grandmother. Or your mother's great-uncle Henry. Of course, this isn't *exactly* true. Because *you* look like yourself, don't you? But it *is* true that you are more like members of your family than you are like other people. This is because of the *particular* kind of sperm and egg that joined to make you. They not only made you resemble your mother and father in many ways, but your grandparents and other relatives as well. And, as a matter of fact, people you've never seen or heard of—your grandparents' parents and their grandparents. And so, far, far back to the time when people began.

Usually, a single egg leaves the ovaries each month. Sometimes, however, two eggs leave at about the same time. Then it may happen that each one unites with a different sperm. If both fertilized eggs grow into babies, they are called twins. One may be a boy and one a girl. They are like any other brother and sister. Or they may both be boys or both girls. Much more rarely, after a fertilized egg starts to grow, it divides into two exactly even parts; then each part can grow into a complete baby. These are called real or true twins. The two are both girls or both boys. They are so much alike that usually even the mother and father cannot easily tell

them apart. Do you know any twin children?

When you were a very tiny infant, you spent practically all of your time sleeping. You stayed awake just long enough to eat—and you woke up to do this every few hours, all day and all night too. And every time you wanted to eat, somebody had to feed you. You couldn't do anything at all about it yourself. For you, like all human babies, were about the most helpless of all living things.

Human babies take a much longer time to grow up than babies of other kinds. Most of the animals you know best, like horses and dogs and cats and cows, are as big as their parents by the time they are two years old. A two-year-old dog can roam over the neighborhood all day long and take good care of himself. But a two-year-old baby cannot. As soon as it is born, a kitten can climb around its mother looking for the places to

suck her milk. A baby has to be held up to its mother's breast to nurse. Or if it nurses from a bottle, someone has to hold the bottle and put the nipple in the baby's mouth. A baby calf can stand on its own legs—even if

they are pretty wobbly—the first day it is born. You know it is a long time, often a whole year, before a baby can stand up.

That's how it is that for a long time after that great day when you were born, you couldn't do much more for yourself than breathe and eat—and grow. But every day you got bigger and stronger. And every day you became a little more able to make your muscles move the way you wanted them to. After a while you could turn your head to look at someone you heard coming into the room. Pretty soon you could smile at your mother and father, or anyone who looked at you. But it took a while before you could reach for a toy or hold your own bottle so that you could drink from it. Or laugh out loud when other children played with you.

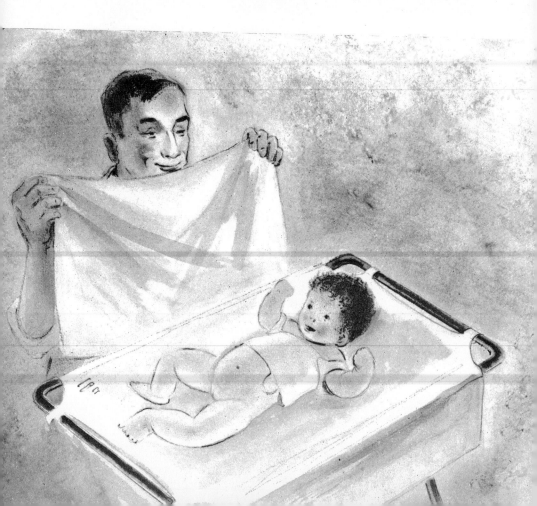

By the time your first birthday came around and you were one year old, you could pull yourself up to stand in your crib or your play pen. You could creep around on the floor and you could grab at everything you saw and get into everything you could reach. But you were still a baby.

Do you remember when you said Da-da instead of Daddy? Choo-choo instead of train? When you could ride a kiddy car but not a bike? When you had to cry for something you wanted because you couldn't say the words to ask for it?

Now you are big and can do a great many things for yourself. You have grown and changed in very many

ways. Because it is not only our bodies that grow and change. Our feelings grow and change, too, and we learn to understand more and more.

When you were a baby, you wanted to be near your mother all the time. Maybe you cried when she left you with someone else. Now, you're just as happy playing away from home at a friend's house, aren't you?

First you needed to feel close mostly to your mother and father. Now you also enjoy feeling close to your friends. That's what I mean by saying that your feelings change as you grow older.

As we get older, our bodies get larger and stronger. They also change in shape. You are able to do many more things with your body than you could do when you were a baby. Your feelings grow and change too. When we are still very young, we begin to notice, and to wonder about our bodies, and about other people's bodies.

I once knew a little girl who felt terribly cheated because her brother had a penis that showed. And so far as she could make out, she had nothing at all. This made her feel that boys got everything and that girls weren't very important. However, her brother felt cheated too, even though he had a penis. *He* felt that girls had all the luck; when they grew up they could have babies but boys couldn't. Of course you know now how very important each is in his or her own way.

Human beings keep on learning and growing for a much longer time than other animals do. As they grow up, boys and girls understand more with their minds and their feelings than any other animals do. Men and women can read and write and think well enough to make up stories and songs and invent airplanes. They can also feel a love for their children and for their husbands and wives that no other animals can. So, human beings live in families of fathers and mothers and children together.

You are growing and changing in your body and in your feelings all the time. In a few years, when you are twelve, thirteen, or fourteen, you will begin to grow even more quickly than you do now. That is the time when boys' bodies begin to change their shape and grow more like men's bodies, and girls' bodies come to be more like women's bodies.

As boys and girls become more grown-up, their feelings become more grown-up too. They begin to think about the changes in their bodies and about each other. They like to have dates with each other and go to dances and parties together. They are growing out of younger ways of loving, just as you grew out of needing your mother near you all the time. And they begin to

wonder about grown-up ways of loving. When they get
to be young men and women, they feel grown-up enough
to get married. It isn't until then that they are able to
give children of their own all the kinds of love and care
that children need.

Have you ever felt that good warm feeling of being close and together with other people? Of course you have. You have thrown your arms around your mother and hugged her tight, feeling very close to her. You love it when your father tucks you into bed at night and gives you a goodnight kiss.

And when your family does something together that's fun, what you've enjoyed is the feeling of all of you being close and being happy together.

When people are married, they feel very close to each other. A married man and woman feel this closeness with their hearts, and they also feel a special closeness with their bodies. They join their bodies together because they love each other. When they join their bodies, the egg and sperm can melt together. That is how the sperm and egg can stop being two separate things and become one new thing—which is the beginning of a baby.

When a man and woman have children together, parents and children together become another kind of new thing. *This* new thing is a family. In families, love surrounds the children who grow up in them—just as love surrounds the joining of the sperm and the egg.

Now, you already know how the story goes on from there. You know how the egg and the sperm melt together. You know how the tiny, tiny dot begins to grow. You know how it changes from a little egg that could hardly be seen, and grows bigger, and changes into a baby inside the mother. And then you know how the baby is born, and how it grows from a tiny little thing in its crib to be a boy or girl as big as you are.

And you are still growing. Little boys and girls become big boys and girls. Then they become men and women, and get married and have children of their own. Their children grow up and have more children, and *they* have children—and so on and on like a story that never comes to an end.

And what I told you is all part of the same wonderful story—the most wonderful story in the world—the *real, true* story of how you were born.

It's such an interesting story that we always want to know more about it. When I was a little girl, I asked many, many questions. And when I became a mother and told my children the story, they asked me many questions. You'll have questions, too. As you grow older, you'll want to understand more about yourself, your body, and your feelings. You'll keep right on asking your father and mother to tell you more and more of this wonderful story.